# **Pancakes and Crepes:**

*The Best 50 Pancake Recipes to Your Table*

## Table of contents:

Introduction

Pancakes with avocado, caviar and red fish

Pancakes "Sun rays"

Pancakes "family"

Hepatic tender pancakes with mushroom filling

Pancakes with milk and cream

Corn pancakes with salsa from pears and avocados

Creamy pancakes

Kataf - Arabian pancakes

Pancakes in baskets

Custard pancakes with yoghurt with "smart" sauce

Pancakes stuffed with yogurt

Omelets pancake with meat

Pancakes on the water (very tasty)

Rice pancakes stuffed with fried radish

Rye pancakes with a sauce of green onions, cilantro, sour cream and red caviar

Thick Norwegian pancakes with raspberry jam

Pancake with pate filling

Pancake pie with chicken and mushrooms

Pancake cake with cranberry cream

Pancakes from custard batter

Thin pancakes with buttermilk (with filling and not only)

Buckwheat pancakes

Eating pancakes on potato broth

Pancakes with apples

Rye pancakes "The Borodino"

Baghrir - Moroccan pancakes

Moroccan semolina pancakes on yeast

Buckwheat pancakes

Russian pancakes (yeast)

Pancakes with caviar and salmon

Pancakes with yeast

Yeast pancakes

Pancakes with zucchini and whole wheat flour

Millet pancakes (lean)

Pancakes "Triple Pleasure"

Semolina pancakes with cottage cheese and honey-berry sauce

Pancakes with chestnut flour and greens

Oat pancakes with banana

Pancakes made of oatmeal

Breton pancakes

Pancakes with corn flour

Lenten pancakes

Pancakes with oat flakes and sour cream

Delicious pancakes

Rye-wheat pancakes

Cheese pancakes with pineapple

Thin pancakes from oatmeal porridge

Cottage cheese pancakes with raisins

Yeast pancakes with sour milk

American pancakes

# Introduction

If before you have never baked pancakes, then, having met this wonderful book, be sure to learn how to prepare this delicious dish. The book will help you even become a real professional pancake case. In it you will find both simple enough and original recipes for their preparation. There are many different recipes for all kinds of pancakes and casseroles, in former times very popular because of their taste and special nourishment. You can experiment on your own by choosing new original sauces and fillings to your casseroles and pancakes. In addition, you probably want to surprise the household and guests with any new drinks. The recipes of the latter are also set out in the pages of this book.

# Pancakes with avocado, caviar and red fish

## Ingredients:
- curd cream "Rama"
- avocado ripe
- clove of garlic
- lemon or lime
- fresh cucumber
- sliced salmon - 50g
- salmon roe - 50g
- greens for decoration

For pancakes:
- 1 tbsp. flour
- 2 tbsp. milk
- 2 eggs
- 1 tsp sugar, a pinch of salt
- 2 tablespoons vegetable oil

## Preparation:
Avocado peel off. Knead together with curd cream until smooth. Sprinkle a lot of juice with lemon or lime. Add a tiny clove of garlic. Salt. Lubricate this mass of pancakes. Decorate the bottom of the dish with a thinly sliced cucumber. On top of the cucumber put a slice of red fish, obliquely cut pancakes, cut the pancakes with a spoonful of red caviar and decorate with a sprig of dill.

# Pancakes "Sun rays"

## Ingredients:
- 1 egg
- 150 ml. milk
- 50 ml. water
- a pinch of salt
- 1 tbsp. sugar
- 50 grams of almonds
- 100 grams of flour
- 1 \ 2 tsp. turmeric
- 100 grams of cheese with mold
- 4 tbsp. l. cottage cheese 7%
- 100 grams of cream 35%
- honey natural

## Preparation:
The egg whipped with a pinch of salt. She added milk, water, sugar and once again whipped.
Almond ground into powder and added it to the total mass, the same sifted flour. I really like the color that gives turmeric, tried to add it, it turned out a very beautiful dough. It baked from it 6 pancakes, turned out to be very thin, but at the same time they do not tear. While they were cooling they made a stuffing: cheese with mildew, cottage cheese and cream stirred well, and frayed through a sieve, it is possible to mix a blender, pasty state.
Take the pancake, evenly apply the filling. Carefully wrap it, place it for 10 minutes in the freezer, so that it's evenly cut and beautifully cut. Serve to the table with natural honey and honey nuts, as well as a glass of good white wine.

# Pancakes "family"

## Ingredients:
- starch- 250g
- flour- 250g
- milk- 250g
- mineral water - 250g
- eggs - 4 pieces.
- yeast dry - flat teaspoon
- sugar-1st.
- salt-pinch
- sunflower oil - 4 tbsp.

## Preparation:
1. Combine the mint with the starch and yeast and sift.
2. Split eggs into a bowl and whisk them with a whisk.
3. In a large bowl we connect all the products, carefully mixing them, breaking all the lumps.
4. Let the dough rest for 30 minutes.
5. At the test I bake thin pancakes. I do not lubricate the scrotum, so, as the composition of the test includes sunflower oil.

# Hepatic tender pancakes with mushroom filling

## Ingredients:
For pancakes:
- 0.5 kg of chicken liver
- 4 eggs
- 100 g of milk
- 4 tbsp. flour
- salt, pepper to taste

Filling:
- 400 g of champignons
- 1 medium onion
- 1 medium carrot
- 4 tbsp. mayonnaise

## Preparation:
First of all, we prepare the filling. My mushrooms, we clean the hats and cut them into cubes. Let's cut a little onion, carrot three on a small grater. Fry mushrooms with the addition of 1 tbsp. of sunflower oil. When the liquid evaporates, add a ray. After the onion has become a transparent carrot turn. We fry our stuffing for another 5-10 minutes and set aside to cool.

Liver washed, cut into pieces. I can twist the meat grinder, but I use a blender (an indispensable assistant in the kitchen). All the ingredients for pancakes are placed in the container for the blender, once or twice and the dough is ready. I added 2 tbsp. to the dough sunflower oil, so as not to lubricate the frying pan. Fry pancakes. It turns out 12 pancakes. In the already cooled stuffing, add 4 tbsp. of mayonnaise, mix and stuff pancakes. For every pancake goes slightly more than 1 filling. Filling smeared half the pancake and wrapped, slightly bending the edges. We send it to the fridge for at least an hour and can be served to the table. When served, you can decorate a plate with lettuce leaves and put a pancake with pancakes.

## Pancakes with milk and cream

### Ingredients:
- Milk 3.2% (hot) - 200 ml
- Cream 20% - 200 ml
- Eggs - 3 pieces
- Flour - 7 tbsp.
- Sugar powder - 2 tbsp.
- A pinch of salt
- Sunflower oil - 1 tbsp.
- Sauce for every taste

### Preparation:
Beat the eggs. Add the cream and beat again. Gradually, continuously interfering, sift flour. Add sugar powder and a pinch of salt. Pour in hot milk. Add the oil and mix. The dough turns out to be quite liquid, so bake them on a very well heated frying pan (you can oil it). Serve with your favorite sauce. I used maple syrup.

# Corn pancakes with salsa from pears and avocados

## Ingredients:
For corn pancakes:
- 2 eggs
- 250 ml of milk
- 2 glass of flour (approximately, it may take less)
- 1 can of canned corn
- 1 tsp sugar
- 1 teaspoon of baking powder
- a pinch of salt
- 3-4 feathers of green onions
- 3 tbsp. oil

For salsa:
- 1 ripe avocado
- juice from half a lemon
- 1 pear, preferably hard varieties (I have a "Conference")
- 4 feathers of green onions
- 10 pcs cherry tomato or 1 plain tomato
- 1 green chili pepper (I did not put it, I forgot)
- salt to taste
- black pepper to taste

## Preparation:
Egg whisk with sugar and salt, pour half a glass of milk, whisk, add flour with baking powder, to interfere with that there were no lumps, add the rest of the milk and stir well the dough, it should be thinner than the pancakes, but thicker than but pancakes, add dough oil, finely chopped green onions and corn (liquid pre-merge). Warm up pan, smear oil (grease only once, then it is not necessary), with a spoon to spread the batter, and bake again equate pancakes with two to the blush. Elan lubricate each pancake butter. Cover pancakes, not to cool down. A yet to make the salsa:

Avocado cut in half, remove the pit, remove the pulp with a spoon and cut into cubes, sprinkle with lemon juice, pear washed, peeled, cored and cut into cubes, too, sprinkle with lemon juice. Tomatoes scalded with boiling water, peel and finely chop, chop the onion, chili grind previously removing the seeds (I cooked without chili), mix all the ingredients, season with black pepper and salt, add lemon juice to taste, mix.

## Creamy pancakes

**Ingredients:**
- wheat flour - 4 tbsp.
- flour pancake - 4 tablespoons
- eggs - 4 pcs.
- milk - 200 ml
- cream (22%) - 100 ml
- sugar - 3 tbsp.
- vanilla sugar - 1 pack.
- salt - 0.5 tsp.
- light beer (I had Reds) - 2 tablespoons
- vegetable oil - 2 tbsp.
- butter - for baking and lubricating ready-made pancakes

**Preparation:**

Eggs beat with salt, sugar and vanilla sugar, until the mixture brightens, add flour, milk and cream. Then the vegetable oil, knead the dough until smooth. After that, add beer to the dough, cover with food film and put it in the refrigerator for at least an hour.

Bake in a hot frying pan, after which each pancake to grease with melted butter.

# Kataf - Arabian pancakes

## Ingredients:
Kataef:
- 1 cup of wheat flour + 2 tbsp. corn flour
- 1 1/4 cup of milk
- 1 tbsp. baking powder
- 1 tbsp. vanilla sugar

Filling:
- 200 g of Philadelphia cheese, or you can use curds without grains
- 1 tbsp. sour cream
- 2 tsp. powdered sugar
- blueberry or cherry jam

## Preparation:
Mix the "Philadelphia" cheese or grated cottage cheese with sour cream and powdered sugar until smooth, creamy consistency. Set aside.

In a small bowl, sift the flour, sugar and baking powder; mix with wire whisk. On high heat, heat a large frying pan with a thick bottom. Pour the milk into a bowl. Gradually sift the mixture of flour, sugar and baking powder, all the while interfering with the whisk. The dough will be slightly thicker than the usual pancakes.

No letting the test take a second to rest, lay out 1 tbsp. on a very hot frying pan, greased with vegetable oil. Now we follow the pancake very carefully. As soon as all the bubbles burst, the dough made of smooth and shiny becomes matte - the pancake is ready. Do not overdo it, otherwise it will become like a waffle - fragile and crunchy, which is bad for the folding of the petal - it just breaks.

Immediately, without wasting any time and not letting it cool down, we spread the kataef on the cutting board and on one side connect the ends with two fingers for a few seconds. It will take no more than a few seconds and the form will hold. Bake all the pancakes in this way. Then fill them with cheese or curd mass, on top of which lay out a few berries from jam.

# Pancakes in baskets

## Ingredients:
For two pancakes:
- 1 small egg
- 2 tablespoons wheat flour
- 1 tablespoon corn flour
- 0.5 tablespoons corn oil
- 1 tablespoon of water
- A small piece of boiled beet
- A pinch of salt
- 0.5 teaspoon of sugar.
- A piece of butter to lubricate the frying pan and forms for baking

For filling:
- 2 sausages
- Four eggs
- Half fresh tomato
- Green onions

## Preparation:
1. Whip all ingredients for pancakes with a whisk.
2. Grate a small piece of boiled beet on a small grater.
3. Preheat pancake pan, oil it with oil. It is also profusely to grease two forms for large cupcakes (or rum baba) with butter.
4. We bake pancakes ONLY ONE SIDE.
5. Transfer the pancake into the mold not baked side down.
6. Fry in sauce pan sausages cut into circles and put them on the bottom of a pancake basket.
7. In a pancake basket we spread a tomato, cut into a circle, we drive two eggs into a basket, salt.
8. Bake our breakfast in the oven for about 15 minutes at a temperature of 190 degrees. After taking it out, sprinkle with herbs and serve it to the table.

# Custard pancakes with yoghurt with "smart" sauce

## Ingredients:
- 2 eggs
- 300 g yogurt
- 250 ml of milk
- 10 tbsp. flour
- 250 boiling water
- 3 tbsp. sugar
- 1 tsp. baking powder
- salt
- vegetable oil
- 1 glass berries (I had a red currant)
- 0,5 glass walnuts
- 1 tbsp. granulated sugar
- a little lemon peel (I used dry)

## Preparation:
Beat eggs with sugar and salt, mix with milk. Add yogurt, beat up a little. Enter the flour, mix well (the consistency turns the dough as a thick sour cream). Add the baking powder and add the boiling water. Mix. Bake in a heated frying pan, greased with vegetable oil on both sides. Served with sauce. For sauce (if you use frozen berries, then pre-defrost), berry the berries with sugar. Chop the nuts in a blender and mix with the berries.

# Pancakes stuffed with yogurt

## Ingredients:
- 1 cup of flour (glass 240 ml)
- 1 cup kefir
- 1 cup of boiling water
- 0.5 teaspoons of salt
- 1 tbsp. of sugar
- 2 eggs
- 0.5 teaspoons of soda
- 2 tbsp. vegetable oil
- for serving 2 servings
- 1 orange
- dried fruits at will (raisins, dried apricots, cranberries, prunes)
- 150g curd cheese
- 2 tbsp. honey or jam

## Preparation:
1. Eggs beat with salt until a small foam. Continue to beat the pour boiling water. The weight will be doubled. Then pour in kefir.
2. Then add sifted flour with soda. Add butter and sugar last. All is good to shake.
3. Fry the pancakes in a heated frying pan.
4. For submission we need 2 pancakes. First cut into 4 parts. These are the wings of a butterfly. On a plate to spread quarters, in one part wrap the orange slice. The other edge to collect as a fan. The second pancake cut into halves, roll into a tube and form an oval, the torso of a butterfly. The trunk is filled with cheese. Decorate with dried fruits and pour with honey.

# Omelets pancake with meat

## Ingredients:
- Eggs 10 pieces
- 5 tablespoons flour
- milk 1.5 cups
- water 1.5 cups
- stuffing 1 kg
- carrot 2-3 average pieces
- green onion
- salt, pepper, mayonnaise, ketchup, sunflower oil

## Preparation:
We boil the carrots, three on a large grater. Ray of the rays. We beat eggs with milk, water and salt. Add the flour and thoroughly mix everything to a homogeneous mass. (that would not have lumps.) Then in the finished grated we add grated carrots and onions. Let's stand for about 10 minutes.
Before baking in the dough, add about 2-3 tablespoons of sunflower oil.
Bake pancake, after turning it increases in volume. Ready pancake spread on a large dish and on the edge we put stuffing. We wrap while warm. We put it on a sheet. Prepare the sauce: mayonnaise and ketchup, mix pepper with warm boiled water. Fill pancakes and put in the oven. Bake at a temperature of 180, 20-25 minutes.

# Pancakes on the water (very tasty)

## Ingredients:
- 0.5 L of warm water
- 2 eggs
- 3 tablespoons vegetable oil
- 0.5 teaspoons baking powder
- 1.5 cups of flour
- salt (to taste)

## Preparation:
Mix flour with baking powder. Add half of the water to the flour and mix well. Then add whipped eggs, salt and sunflower oil, again mix everything well. Then add the remaining water to the dough and knead the dough to the consistency of the liquid sour cream. Dough better beaten with a mixer or whisk. When baking the first pancake, you need to lubricate the frying pan with sunflower oil, then do not lubricate.

## Rice pancakes stuffed with fried radish

### Ingredients:
- Radish green - 1 pc.
- Shrimp - 500 g
- Soy sauce - 1 tbsp.
- Honey - 1 tsp.
- Vegetable oil
- Rice paper
- Seasonings for fish and seafood, garlic, a little bit of chili

### Preparation:
Radish chop thin strips, fry in vegetable oil, at the end of frying add a mixture of soy sauce with honey. Remove from the frying pan a "leaky spoon". Shrimp clean, quickly fry in a sauce from the frying of radish. Combine the radish with prawns, seasonings, mix well.
Sheets of rice paper moisten in warm water and wrap the filling in them, as in ordinary thin pancakes. Fry the pancakes on both sides until golden brown.

# Rye pancakes with a sauce of green onions, cilantro, sour cream and red caviar

## Ingredients:
- 100 g of rye flour
- 100 g of wheat flour
- 1 tbsp. sugar
- 3 eggs
- 0.5 h salt
- 400 ml of milk
- 2 tablespoons sour cream
- 0.5 h l dry yeast
- vegetable oil

For sauce:
- 100 ml of sour cream
- 50 g of green onion
- 30 grams of coriander
- 1 tbsp. vegetable oil
- 1/4 lemon juice
- 1 tsp. of mustard (preferably Dijon)
- 1.5 tbsp. red caviar
- salt
- pepper

## Preparation:
Eggs beat up with milk, 2 tablespoons of sour cream, sugar, salt. Yeast will dissolve in 1 tbsp. of warm water. Add to the egg-milk mixture. Sift both types of flour and pour into the egg-milk mixture constantly stirring with a whisk. A homogeneous liquid mass should be obtained. Leave on the table for 20-30 minutes. Spread out the pancake pan (better cast iron), grease it with vegetable oil and bake pancakes in the usual way. Cilantro and green onions to wash, dry and coarsely chop. In a blender, chopped onions and cilantro, sour cream, sunflower oil, lemon juice and mustard. The resulting mass of a spoon is mixed with red caviar. Salt and pepper to taste. Lubricate the finished pancakes with sauce, curtail and serve.

## Thick Norwegian pancakes with raspberry jam

### Ingredients:
- A half liter of fat thick yogurt
- 2 eggs
- 75-100g of sugar
- 2/3 tsp soda
- 1/2 tsp. ammonium carbonate
- 450 ml of flour
- olive oil or butter for frying

### Preparation:
Mix the dry ingredients. Lightly beat the egg, add kefir, mix and add to the dry mixture. Then we give the floor for an hour to rest the test. We pour one cup on the center of the oiled frying pan, that would turn out a plump pancake the size of a small saucer. We bake. Let's cool a bit and spread the jam on top.

# Pancake with pate filling

## Ingredients:
For pancakes:
- egg-4 pcs.
- milk-800 ml.
- mayonnaise-3 tbsp.
- flour-10-15 tablespoons
- sunflower oil for frying pancakes.

For paté:
- Chicken liver -800 gr.
- onion-2 bulbs.
- Boiled egg-2 pcs.
- cream 35% fat-100 ml.
- dried rosemary-1 tsp
- Oregano Dried-1 tsp
- mixture of peppers (white, pink, black) -to taste
- salt to taste
- sunflower-oil for frying

## Preparation:
Knead out of all the ingredients for the pancakes batter. According to the consistency of the dough should be like a thin sour cream. Bake pancakes. (I got 12 pieces in a frying pan with a diameter of 24 cm). Liver and chopped onion on a sunflower oil until golden brown. Season the liver with salt and dried herbs, add the cream and simmer until the liver is ready. Punch the blender to a homogeneous mass of liver and boiled eggs. In a split form (24 cm in diameter), put the pancake on top of the whole pancake spread the paste with a layer of 0.5 cm (if the pate is too thick, you can add the right amount of mayonnaise). Do the same procedure with all the pancakes. The top layer should be a pancake. Lubricate it with mayonnaise, to form a golden crust when baked. Bake a cake for 15-20 minutes in an oven heated to 160-180 degrees.

## Pancake pie with chicken and mushrooms

### Ingredients:
- Pancakes - kefir - 1 liter
- egg - 2 pcs.
- flour - 2-3 tbsp.
- salt, sugar to taste

  Filling:
- chicken fillet - 0,5 kg
- mushrooms - 200 g.
- cheese - 150 g.
- onion - 2 pcs.
- some green onion feathers
- sour cream - 250 g.
- one egg for lubrication

### Preparation:
Flour, kefir, eggs, salt and sugar mixed in a combine. Bake thin pancakes. Chicken fillet boil, cut into small pieces. Mushrooms (I have champignons, but can be any) fry, add onions and quarter-rings and fry a little more. In the chicken filling, add crushed green onions and a couple of tablespoons of broth, mix. In the mushrooms add onion grated cheese and mix too. Both that and another to salt and pepper. Lubricate the form with oil. Place in it three or four pancakes fan from the center, so that the sides of the form are closed (leave three pancakes at once for the top of the pie), grease with sour cream. Place the stuffing from the chicken. Cover with one or two pancakes. They again grease sour cream, place the filling of mushrooms. Turn the pancakes and stuffing, until the pancakes or stuffing are over))). Top cover with pancakes and a fan. Top the pie with a beaten egg. Bake in the oven for 20-25 minutes.

# Pancake cake with cranberry cream

## Ingredients:
For pancakes:
- Water (1.5 cups)
- Wheat flour (3 tablespoons)
- Rye flour (3 tablespoons)
- Rye bran (1 tablespoon)
- egg (2 pcs.)
- A pinch of salt
- Soda (at the tip of the knife)

For cream:
- cranberry (1/2 cup)
- Water (1 glass)
- Egg (1 pc.)
- Cognac (1 tsp)
- Cinnamon (1/2 tsp)
- Sugar (8-10 tsp)
- Condensed milk (2 tsp)
- Butter (50 grams)
- Flour (2 tablespoons)

## Preparation:
Cooking pancakes:
The volume ratio of the ingredients is approximate, so you need to regulate their content according to the appearance of the test. The dough should not be thick, and should flow well in the pan. You just need to mix all the ingredients: first the egg, salt, flour, bran and soda. I baked pancakes without oil on a cast-iron frying pan, so they were slightly dried. Pancakes can be made in different sizes, reducing them to make the cake a pyramidal shape.

Cream preparation:
It is necessary to wash the cranberries and cook in a glass of water about 10-15 minutes before the berries give all the juice. Then strain the liquid to separate from the pulp. In a separate plate mix the egg, flour, sugar (the amount of sugar at your discretion, my cake turned out not very sweet), condensed milk and a little got cranberry liquid (after its cooling, so that the egg white does not curl up). Then pour the resulting mixture into the cranberry liquid and put it on a slow fire. We stir and wait until it thickens. In the process of stirring, add cognac and cinnamon. After

thickening, remove the cream from the plate and let it cool. Add a softened creamy little.

Completion:

Spread out layer by layer every pancake and grease with cream. You can leave one pancake to form the rims (you can and without them). We decorate with cranberries on top.

## Pancakes from custard batter

### Ingredients:
- 1 liter. fermented milk products (I have curdled milk)
- 2 eggs
- 3 tablespoons sugar
- Vanilla on the tip of a knife or vanilla sugar
- 1/2 tsp. salt
- 1 tsp soda, hydrated vinegar
- 3 tablespoons vegetable oil
- flour
- 100 gr. vodka (for more laced pancakes

### Preparation:
Eggs beat up with sugar, add vanilla, if there is vodka, salt. Add the curdled milk, stir and pour in flour so much to make the dough, like a pancake. Then put soda, slaked with vinegar, vegetable oil, mix again. Pour boiling water into the dough to make the dough thick as liquid, like thin pancakes. Bake as usual.

# Thin pancakes with buttermilk (with filling and not only)

## Ingredients:
For pancakes:
- Flour - 140 gr.
- Buttermilk - 200 ml
- Milk - 250 ml
- Eggs - 2 pcs.
- Salt - ½ tsp.
- Sugar - 1,5 tbsp.
- Vegetable oil - 5 tbsp.

For filling:
- Minced meat - 200 gr.
- Egg - 1 pc.
- Bow - 1 head
- Salt - pinch

Yet:
- Butter - 30-40 gr.
- Butter for frying
- Sausages
- Sour cream and jam for filing
- Syrup

## Preparation:
Buttermilk I did myself: in warm milk added lemon juice and allowed to stand for about 20 minutes. Eggs beat up with sugar and salt. Add milk (warm!) And buttermilk. Mix. Add the oil. Mix. Gradually add the sifted flour, stirring the dough, so that the lumps do not turn out. It should not be a thick dough. Cover it with a film and put it in the refrigerator for at least 2 hours (I had a night!). Get the dough, mix, bake thin pancakes on one side in a well-heated frying pan (I have cast iron, I have not found anything better for baking pancakes!). Prepare the filling: mince fry with onion until rouge. Egg boil and cut. Add to the stuffing, mix everything. The filling is ready. We start to form pancakes: on the toasted side of the blink we put stuffing and little piece of butter. We wrap it. Fry pancakes in a hot frying pan until golden brown.

# Buckwheat pancakes

## Ingredients:

- Water 300ml
- Wheat flour 12 tbsp. with a slide
- Yeast dry (I have "Saf-levure") 1 tsp.
- Sugar 2 tsp.
- Boiled buckwheat 1 glass
- Milk 300ml
- Vegetable oil

## Preparation:

Prepare the yeast according to the instructions on the package, my need to be soaked in water, some simply added to the flour. Sift flour with salt. Combine warm water, flour, sugar, yeast, stir until the lumps disappear, cover with a towel or a film and put in a warm place. The dough should go up 2-3 times and get a good start.
Buckwheat (not from the refrigerator), whisk in a blender until smooth, if necessary, you can add a little warm water. Milk bring to a boil, but do not boil.
In the risen dough add the buckwheat puree, stir and immediately brew with boiled milk, stirring with a spoon or spatula, preferably wooden, add 1-2 tablespoons. vegetable oil, another time to mix well and immediately bake pancakes on a hot skillet. I lubricated the oil only for the first 2 portions. If the dough turned out too thick, you can dilute a bit of warm water.

# Eating pancakes on potato broth

## Ingredients:
- About 5 kg of potatoes (for decoction)
- 0.5 liters mineral water soda
- 1 large onion
- 250g. oil (approximately, it can take less)
- flour about 2 cups
- salt to taste
- 1 tsp soda or baking powder

## Preparation:
Boil the peeled potatoes until cooked (until the potatoes are peeled and cut into onions, fried in a medium until golden brown), decoction of the broth (decoction about a little less than a liter), use potatoes at your own discretion, you can chop with fried onion and stuff the pancakes) , salt and pour the flour into a hot broth, quickly stir that there would not be lumps, you should get a dough like a thick sour cream, add soda, and pour soda water, stirring the dough to make the consistency of the pancake dough, add the fried onion with m scrapped, again well stir. Fry pancakes on a well-heated frying pan from both sides, grease the pan once oil, then you do not need to smear, pancakes good shot.

## Pancakes with apples

### Ingredients:
- 1/2 apple
- 80g of vegetable oil
- 2 tablespoons sugar

### Preparation:
Cut the apple, cut into 4 parts, remove the core with a seed box and seeds. Cut the apple into thin slices. In the frying pan, serve butter, melt it over medium heat, pour two tablespoons of sugar and let the sugar completely dissolve in the oil, stirring. Cut the thin apple plastics into a pan in the resulting syrup, fry the minutes 2 on one side and turn over to the other side to fry also minutes 2. In the middle of each pancake put 3 plastic apple, water not a lot of syrup and curtail the roll. If pancakes already cooled, you can warm them in the microwave (which I did) ь rolls on a plate, put slices of apple around rolls, pour everything with syrup.

## Rye pancakes "The Borodino"

### Ingredients:
- 150 g of rye flour
- 50 g of wheat flour
- 2 eggs
- 500 g of yogurt
- 1 tbsp. sugar
- 1 tsp. salt
- 1/2 tsp. soda
- 1 tsp. coriander in beans
- 1 tsp. caraway
- 1 tbsp. vegetable oil in dough + vegetable oil

### Preparation:
Mix rye and wheat flour, salt, sugar. Cumin and coriander grains should be roasted in a dry frying pan and grinded in a mortar. Add to the dry mix and mix. Beat eggs with a whisk, add kefir. To mix. Combine the egg-kefir and dry mixture by stirring constantly so that lumps do not form. Allow to stand for 30 minutes. If a thick dough turns out, then add a little boiled water. Before baking, add soda, stir. Pour in the cooking oil and mix. Pour a little oil on a hot cast-iron frying pan and pour a portion of dough. Furnish pancakes in the usual way on both sides.

## Baghrir - Moroccan pancakes

### Ingredients:
- 300 gr of flour
- 100 gr of mango
- 2 egg yolks
- 1 tbsp. sugar
- 1 tbsp. vegetable oil
- salt
- half a teaspoon ripper
- 10 g yeast
- warm water (you can do on milk)

### Preparation:
Flour, mango, sugar, ripper, salt to mix. Yeast diluted in warm water (about a glass) and let stand. Combine with dry ingredients, add the eggs, mix and let stand for 45 minutes. Add water or warm milk. It took me three glasses, but look at your dough. Maybe more. Add the vegetable oil. Fry on a lightly oiled frying pan ONLY ONE SIDE. In the process of roasting, large holes appear. Serve with honey or something sweet.

# Moroccan semolina pancakes on yeast

## Ingredients:
- 1 tbsp. semolina
- 0.5 tbsp. flour
- 1 tsp without a hill of dry yeast
- 1 tsp baking powder
- 1 tbsp. warm water
- 1 tbsp. warm milk
- 1 tsp salt
- 1 tsp sugar

## Preparation:
In a bowl of a blender, mix, mango, flour, salt, sugar, yeast, baking powder. Gradually introduce a mixture of milk and water. Beat in a blender until smooth. Leave in a warm place for an hour. Before baking, stir the dough. Bake on medium heat on a hot frying pan with plenty of greased vegetable oil (grease before each baking). Bake only on one side!

# Buckwheat pancakes

**Ingredients:**
- Buckwheat flour - 350 gr
- Flour - 150 gr
- Serum - approx. 4 items
- Egg - 3 pieces
- Yeast dry - 5-7 gr
- Salt - 1 tsp.
- Sugar - 1/2 tbsp.
- Butter - 100 gr
- Vegetable oil or slice of fat

**Preparation:**

Both flour sift, mix with salt, sugar, yeast. Melt the butter (it is optional!). Lightly beat eggs, combine with serum and butter. Combine items 2 and 4, carefully mix. In a very warm place give rise (1.5-2 times). Stir and fry, oiling the frying pan with oil or, as is customary in our family, a piece of fat. If butter is added, then grill pancakes of small diameter, so that it is easier to turn and remove.

# Russian pancakes (yeast)

## Ingredients:
- Yeast (fresh, or dry - 2.5 tablespoons) - 50 g
- Salt - 1 tsp.
- Sugar - 2 tbsp.
- Egg of chicken - 4 pieces
- Milk - 5 glass
- Wheat flour - 5 glasses
- Butter (or margarine) butter - 200 g

## Preparation:
First we make a spit. In two glasses of warm milk we brew yeast and add 3 cups of flour. Mix everything well and put it in a warm place for 30-40 minutes. After this time, the opara should increase by about 2 times, salt is added to it, sugar, melted butter, mashed yolks (pre-isolate the yolks from proteins), stir the rest of the flour and gradually add the remaining warm milk. Well, everything is mixed, you can mixer, as the dough is not thick, cover with a clean towel. And we set to approach (before the increase in the test in 2 times). The dough is kneaded and set to walk again. As the dough fits the second time, whip the proteins into a strong foam and add to the dough, mix and leave for 15-20 minutes. Bake pancakes on a hot frying pan (preferably with thick walls, cast iron), greased with vegetable oil, on both sides. I bake a baked pancake with butter and sprinkle with sugar.

## Pancakes with caviar and salmon

### Ingredients:
- Milk - 1 liter
- Egg - 8-9 pieces (depending on the size)
- Flour - 400 g
- Sugar -1-2 tablespoons
- Salt - 1 tsp.
- Soda - 1/4 tsp
- Vegetable oil - 4-5 tbsp.
- Butter - 50 g (if poured into the dough)
- Fish red and caviar - how much do not mind
- Curd cheese 1/2 bath.

### Preparation:
In a convenient container, beat the eggs with the addition of 1/2 part of the flour and 1/4 of the milk - so that there are no lumps. Add sugar, salt and soda. Stir. Gradually add the rest of the flour and milk whilst continuing to beat. Approximately a glass of milk to leave to add after the dough is infused. Leave the dough to "rest" for 40-50 minutes. Stir, if densely in your opinion, then add gradually the remaining milk, vegetable oil. Since I this time pancakes stuffed with fish and caviar, I melted butter and poured into the dough. Bake as usual on a very well heated frying pan with 2 sides. In this case, do not forget to adjust the fire as needed. Finished pancake to grease with curd cheese a little, put on it pieces of fish and roll up a roll. Just put the pancake caviar, but already without cheese.

# Pancakes with yeast

## Ingredients:
- Flour - 330 g
- Egg (50g) - 1 piece
- Sugar - 20 g
- Butter - 25 g
- Milk - 550 g
- Yeast (dry) - 7 g
- Salt - 7 g

## Preparation:
The first step is to prepare the yeast. Milk slightly warmed, pour 100 g and dissolve yeast in it, set aside for 10 minutes. If you want to use fresh yeast, you need 20 g. In the remaining milk (450 g), dissolve salt and sugar, add milk with yeast, stir. Drive in the egg and add the sifted flour, stir. Melt the butter and pour it into the dough, stir it. It turns smooth dough, consistency - liquid sour cream. Put in a warm place for 1 hour, during this time the dough should be mixed a couple of times, "crumble." Bake pancakes from two sides in a heated frying pan with oil.

# Yeast pancakes

## Ingredients:
- Flour - 500 gr
- Water - approx. 700 ml
- Dry yeast - 5-6 gr
- Sugar - 6 tbsp.
- Salt - 1 tsp
- Vegetable oil - 5-6 tbsp.
- Raw potatoes - 1 pc.
- Vegetable oil

## Preparation:
Sift flour, combine with sugar, salt, yeast. Peel potatoes and grate them on the smallest grater (mashed potatoes). Combine water, butter and mashed potatoes. Combine 1 and 3 items, mix well and allow to approach 2 times. Stir and fry, oiling the frying pan. Pancake should be given a good blush, and then turned over to the other side.

# Pancakes with zucchini and whole wheat flour

## Ingredients:
- Glass - 150 ml
- Zucchini pulp - 250 g.
- Kefir - 1.5 tbsp.
- Wheat flour - 1 tbsp.
- Wholemeal flour - 0.5 tbsp.
- Sugar - 1 tsp.
- Eggs - 2 pieces
- Soda - 0.3 tsp.
- Salt - 0.3 tsp.
- Vegetable oil - 1-2 tablespoons

## Preparation:
1. Squash, wash from the skin and seeds, grate on a coarse grater.
2. Mix both types of flour and soda.
3. Eggs shake whisk together with sugar and salt and kefir.
4. Portions sift flour mixture in egg-kefir, each time mixing well.
5. Next in the dough add a grated zucchini, stir.
6. Warm the pancake well with oil.
7. Spread several tablespoons of dough on one pancake.
8. Bake pancakes to a ruddy color on each side.
9. Serve with sour cream.

# Millet pancakes (lean)

## Ingredients:
- a glass of millet flakes
- 3 cups flour
- 5 glasses of water
- 1 packet (11 g) of dry yeast
- 2 tablespoons of sugar
- 1 teaspoon of salt
- 1/2 cup vegetable oil (better with odor)
- vegetable oil for lubricating the frying pan

## Preparation:
Millet flakes pour 3 cups of boiling water, put on fire and cook for about 3 minutes. Then the resulting porridge should be left to cool.
Dilute yeast in 1/3 cup water and 1 teaspoonful. of sugar. Then add the flour to the porridge and mix, add 1 glass of water, salt, sugar and yeast. Then mix thoroughly. Wrap the dough with a towel and leave to go up for 2 hours (I got up in 50 minutes). When the dough rises add 1/2 cup vegetable oil and 1 glass of warm water. To stir thoroughly. Before baking, fry the frying pan with vegetable oil.

# Pancakes "Triple Pleasure"

## Ingredients:
- Flour - 270 gr
- Salt - 1 tsp.
- Sugar - 8 tbsp.
- Cherry - 300 gr
- Cottage cheese - 300 gr
- Apples - 3 pieces
- Cinnamon - 1 tsp.
- Milk - 500 ml
- Vanillin - 0.5 gr
- Egg of chicken - 3 pieces
- Sugar powder - 20 gr
- Sunflower oil - 5 tbsp.

## Preparation:
1. Mix milk, eggs, sugar, salt, flour and sunflower oil.
2. Stir well until the consistency of the liquid sour cream.

We prepare pancakes:

3. Put the frying pan on a small fire.
4. Lubricate the frying pan with sunflower oil.
5. Put the dough on a frying pan with a ladle.
6. Fry the pancake for a few minutes on each side.

Cooking stuffing:

7. Mix sugar, cottage cheese and vanillin.
8. Thoroughly mix the resulting mass.
9. Grate apples on a large grater.
10. Add sugar and cinnamon.
11. Thoroughly mix the resulting mass.
12. We use a fresh or frozen cherry.
13. Remove cherries from the cherry and drain excess juice.

Add the filling to pancakes

14. Lay out the curd filling, roll the pancake by 1/3.
15. Lay out the cherry, sprinkle with sugar, still roll the pancake by 1/3.
16. Lay out the apple filling and roll the pancake completely.
17. Fry the pancake on each side for a minute.

# Semolina pancakes with cottage cheese and honey-berry sauce

## Ingredients:
- Semolina TM Mistral - 3 tbsp.
- Curd fatty homogeneous - 250 gr
- Salt - pinch
- Sugar - 3 tbsp.
- Baking Powder - 0.5 tsp.
- Eggs - 4 pcs small
- Butter - 40 g melted
- Vegetable oil for baking
- Red currant - handful
- Currant black - handful
- Honey liquid - 2 tbsp.
- Berry juice - 4 tbsp.

## Preparation:
1. Eggs, cottage cheese, baking powder, salt, sugar, butter and semolina are very good to stir and leave on the table, so that the lime is slightly swollen, for 10-15 minutes.
2. Heat the frying pan, pour in a little vegetable oil.
3. We spread the dough in small circles.
4. On a slow fire, bake on one side under the lid.
5. Carefully turn over and without the lid bake on the other side quickly - damn it almost bake.
6. Before each pancake, we lightly oil the frying pan with vegetable oil, literally with a tassel - bake it better in a non-stick frying pan.
7. For the sauce mix berries, honey and berry juice mix and adjust to taste.

# Pancakes with chestnut flour and greens

## Ingredients:
- Fermented baked milk- 250 ml
- Kefir 250 ml
- Milk - 300 ml
- Chestnut flour - 1 glass
- Wheat flour - how much dough will take
- Eggs of medium size - 4 pcs.
- Green onions - several feathers
- Dill - several branches
- Salt - black pepper
- Sugar sand - 1 tbsp.
- Baking powder - at the tip of the knife
- Olive oil - 4 tbsp.
- Butter - 3 tbsp.

## Preparation:
1. Mix the mixer with fermented milk, milk, kefir, eggs and chestnut flour until homogeneity. Then add olive oil, salt and pepper to taste, sugar, baking powder on the tip of the knife and mix everything with a mixer again.
2. Wash greens and finely chop, add to the dough.
3. Then gradually add wheat flour and whisk the dough. It should turn out in a consistency, like not fatty sour cream. Not too thick and not too liquid.
4. Next, in a frying pan for baking pancakes, melt 3 tablespoons of butter and quickly pour into the dough intensively stirring, that would the oil disperse evenly.
5. We start baking, oiling the pan with olive oil before frying a fresh pancake. Peach from two sides to blush and pile into a pile.

# Oat pancakes with banana

## Ingredients:
- 1,5-2 tbsp. flour
- 0.5 tbsp. oat flakes (I have fast)
- 50-60 gr. butter
- 2 tsp. baking powder
- 1/3 tsp soda
- 1 ¼ glass milk
- 0.5 tbsp. raisins
- 2 tablespoons brown sugar
- a pinch of salt
- 2 eggs
- 1 large ripe mashed banana (I rubbed it on the grater)

For filing
- maple syrup (I served with wild honey)
- bananas

## Preparation:
Sift in a bowl of flour with baking powder and soda, add sugar, oat flakes, raisins, banana, eggs. Pour in the milk and mix (for a short while, just mix the ingredients), add the melted butter and carefully mix the consistency of very thick cream.
a frying pan for pancakes to heat, grease with vegetable oil (to grease as for pancakes, instead of to water), spread on 1 item of l. dough and oven like pancakes over medium heat (when the edges will grasp to flip over). Grease the pan before each bake of pancakes. Serve with a banana cut into slices and pour over maple syrup.

## Pancakes made of oatmeal

**Ingredients:**
- 1.5 cup warm milk
- 2 pcs. eggs
- 2 tbsp. of sugar
- 1/4 tsp of salt
- 1/4 teaspoons of soda
- 2 tbsp. vegetable oil
- 1 cup oatmeal
- 1/4 cup of plain flour

**Preparation:**
Mix everything with a mixer, let stand for 30 minutes. At first it seems that the dough is liquid, but it will stand and thicken. Then in a heated frying pan bake like ordinary pancakes. If the dough turns out densely, you can dilute it a little with water or milk. Grease pancakes with butter.

## Breton pancakes

**Ingredients:**
- wheat flour 200 gr.
- buckwheat flour 3 tbsp.
- melted butter melted 3 tbsp.
- eggs 2 pcs.
- milk 250 gr.
- salt
- cinnamon 0,5 tsp
- cognac 1 tbsp.
- water

**Preparation:**
We sift the flour into the bowl, make a deepening in the center and pour eggs and milk into it, add salt (a little), knead the dough, pour the water until we get it to the desired consistency (water - about 100 gr), set it aside at least for half an hour, then add cinnamon and cognac and bake thin pancakes in a dry frying pan. I got 12 pieces. Here now the most interesting! If you want to serve biscuits salty, you can wrap them in cheese Roquefort, or another cheese, or shrimp, or ham, missed Philadelphia.

## Pancakes with corn flour

**Ingredients:**
- 500 ml of mineral carbonated water
- 1 cup of wheat flour
- 1 cup of small cornmeal
- 3 eggs
- a pinch of salt
- pinch of sugar
- 3 tablespoons vegetable oil

**Preparation:**
Mix the sifted corn and wheat flour with sugar and salt. Whisk the eggs with whisk and add to the dry mixture. Little by little, we introduce mineral water, not forgetting to stir (the mineral water foams, it should be so). In the dough, add vegetable oil, mix well and leave the dough to rest for 15-20 minutes. Bake pancakes on a hot frying pan on both sides.

## Lenten pancakes

### Ingredients:
For 500 ml of water
- 5 tablespoons (possible with a slide) of sugar
- 0.5 pinch of salt
- 1 tablespoon with a slide of dry yeast
- 4-5 tablespoons vegetable oil
- 3-4 glasses of flour

### Preparation:
We pour warm water, sugar, yeast into the pan, mix everything until dissolution, after pouring in about 4 tablespoons of vegetable oil and pour in flour, so as not to overdo it with flour, the dough should be just a bit thicker than usual pancakes. We put in a warm place, for example a battery, we cover with something warm and we wait when the dough rises at least half. And all you can fry pancakes.

## Pancakes with oat flakes and sour cream

### Ingredients:
- 1 packet of dry yeast (11g)
- 0.5kg of flour
- 200g of oat flakes
- 1L of milk (can be made on water)
- 100g cream
- 3 eggs
- 2 tbsp. vegetable oil
- 2 tbsp. sugar
- 1 tsp. salt (incomplete)
- fat for baking (I baked on vegetable oil)

For cream:
- sour cream 20% fat 200 g
- 3 tbsp. strawberries, wiped with sugar

### Preparation:
Mix yeast with flour. In the flakes pour 0.5 liters of hot milk, add salt, sugar, cream, eggs, vegetable oil, the rest of the milk. Stir well (so that there are no lumps) and allow the dough to stand for 15-20 minutes in a warm place. Bake in a frying pan, oiled in the usual way. For cream, whip the sour cream with the strawberry, rubbed with sugar.

# Delicious pancakes

## Ingredients:
- 220 gr of wheat flour
- 300 ml of serum
- 2 eggs
- 2 tsp. baking powder
- 1 tbsp. sugar
- a pinch of salt
- 2 tablespoons butter

## Preparation:
Mix flour with baking powder and salt, sift. Add sugar. And all the best mix, you can whip. In a separate bowl, whisk eggs lightly, pour in the serum. Mix the flour with liquidity with a crown or mixer, until the lumps disappear. Now pour in the melted butter (you can and vegetable). It is good to heat up a frying pan, to grease with oil only once (before the first pancake). Pour the dough on half the ladle, fry on one side until the unprocessed side is covered with small bubbles. It's time to turn the pancake. On the second side, fry literally for half a minute.

# Rye-wheat pancakes

## Ingredients:
1 glass rye flour
1 tbsp. wheat flour
2 eggs
2.5 tbs. kefir
2 tbsp. sugar
1 h l salt
1 tbsp. vegetable oil + baking oil

## Preparation:
Sift both kinds of flour. Mix with sugar and salt. Eggs beat up. Introduce the eggs into the flour mixture, kefir, stirring constantly. Add 1 tbsp. vegetable oil and mix. Preheat a cast-iron frying pan with vegetable oil. Pour the dough and bake pancakes in the usual way.

## Cheese pancakes with pineapple

**Ingredients:**
- 250 g canned pineapple
- 200 g high fat sour cream
- 1 + 1/3 tbsp. wheat flour
- 150 g of Russian cheese
- 2-2.5 glass of milk
- 2 eggs
- 1 h l of sugar
- oil for frying

**Preparation:**
Separate the proteins from the yolks. Grate the cheese on a fine grater. Mix the yolks with a fork with milk. Egg and milk mixture stirring gradually pour into the flour. Add the cheese, sugar. Whip the whites and mix with the dough. Bake some small pancakes. Drain the juice from the canned pineapple, chop the pineapples finely and mix with sour cream. Fill the pancakes with pancakes and roll them with rolls.

## Thin pancakes from oatmeal porridge

### Ingredients:
- 1 cup oatmeal (porridge in bags with fruit additives, which should not be cooked)
- 2 cups of milk
- 2 eggs
- 2 tbsp. sugar
- slightly salt and baking powder

### Preparation:
Soak the oatmeal in hot milk and cool. Grind the resulting mass with a blender. Add eggs, sugar, salt and baking powder. Beat with a mixer. If it is too liquid, you can add a few spoons of flour. Pour in the cooking oil, mix. Bake delicious pancakes in a frying pan.

## Cottage cheese pancakes with raisins

### Ingredients:
- Milk 400 ml.
- Curd cheese 100 gr.
- Eggs 3 pcs.
- Raisins 100 gr.
- Sugar 4 tbsp.
- A little salt
- Vanilla sugar-1 sachet
- Soda 0.5 tsp
- Flour, how many will take

### Preparation:
Cottage cheese whip with a mixer. To finish all the ingredients except flour and raisins, again whisk again. Render raisins and sprinkle a little flour, mixing with a spoon, until the cream is sour. Frying pan is well heated. Blancs fry in sunflower oil, until golden crust on both sides. Ready pancakes I store in a container or bag, then they are always soft. Serve with your favorite jam.

## Yeast pancakes with sour milk

### Ingredients:
- Water boiled 6 tbsp.
- Sour milk 2 tbsp.
- Yeast, fresh, 50 g
- Sugar 3-4 tablespoons
- Salt to taste
- Flour about 5 tbsp.
- Vegetable oil 2 tbsp.

### Preparation:
Yeast diluted in warm water. Add sugar, stir. Pour the curdled milk, salt, then flour. The dough should be a kefir consistency.
Stir well until smooth, without lumps. Put the dough in a warm place, that it would rise. It took me about 30 minutes. We should have foam on the surface. Stir the vegetable oil. For the first pancake to grease the frying pan, for the others it is not necessary. Bake delicate pancakes not large in the usual way in a well-heated frying pan.

# American pancakes

## Ingredients:
- 1 cup of flour
- 1 cup kefir
- 1 egg
- 1 tbsp. sugar
- 0.5 tsp salt
- 1 tsp soda
- 1 tbsp. vegetable oil

## Preparation:
1. Mix dry ingredients: flour, sugar, salt, soda.
2. Yolk detached from the protein and mix with kefir.
3. Pour kefir into a bowl of flour and stir so that there are no lumps.
4. Then beat the protein into a thick foam and mix with the resulting dough .
5. Add the vegetable oil.
6. Feat on low heat without oil.

Copyright: Published in the United States by Jane Willan/ © Jane Willan All Rights Reserved. No part of this publication or the information in it may be quoted from or reproduced in any form by means such as printing, scanning, photocopying or otherwise without prior written permission of the copyright holder. Disclaimer and Terms of Use: Effort has been made to ensure that the information in this book is accurate and complete, however, the author and the publisher do not warrant the accuracy of the information, text and graphics contained within the book due to the rapidly changing nature of science, research, known and unknown facts and internet. The Author and the publisher do not hold any responsibility for errors, omissions or contrary interpretation of the subject matter herein. This book is presented solely for motivational and informational purposes only.